To my fellow Swifties,

Many of us have loved her from the start, but some of us a... ...the world of being a Swiftie. Whether you've been a fan for 17 years or 17 minutes, I'm happy you're here!

I'm one of the fans who's been here for 17 years. Her debut album was one of the first cd's I ever bought for myself as a kid. I grew up on Taylor's songs, and they have been the soundtrack to so many big (and small) moments in my life. From navigating the ups and downs of middle school, dealing with mean girls, experiencing my first love and heartbreak, to the day I welcomed my first daughter into the world, there's a Taylor Swift song that captures every memory.

Most recently, The Tortured Poets Department has been a deeply cathartic album for me to listen to as I have had to navigate single motherhood. I've been raising my two little girls on Taylor Swift music, too, and I'm proud to say I've added 2 more Swifties to the pack.

I really poured my heart into this coloring book and I hope that as you go through the pages, you'll be transported back to your own memories - the one's where her music was your soundtrack, too. While drawing each of these designs, it's been that way for me.

I am so happy this book it has found its way to you. I hope you enjoy it, I made it just for us!

Love,

Lou Lou Lane

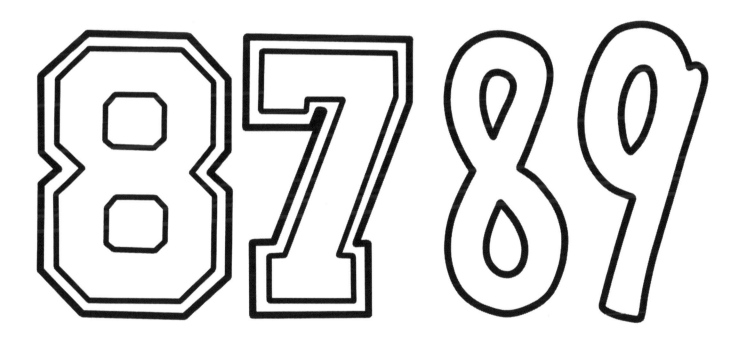

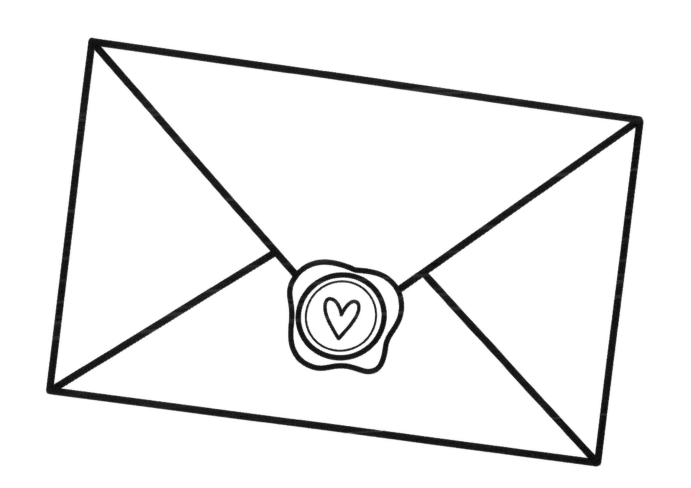

FEARLESS
TAYLOR'S VERSION

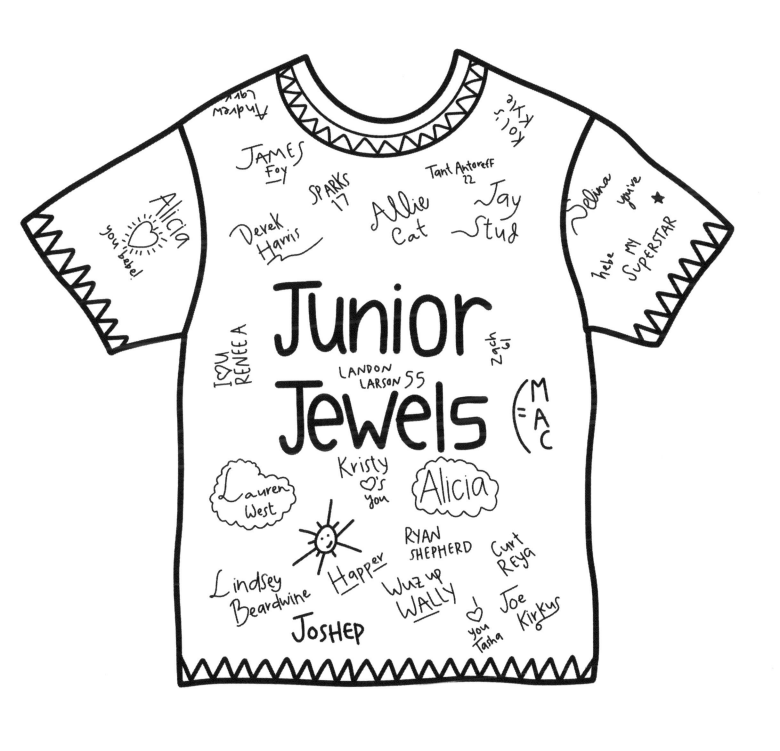

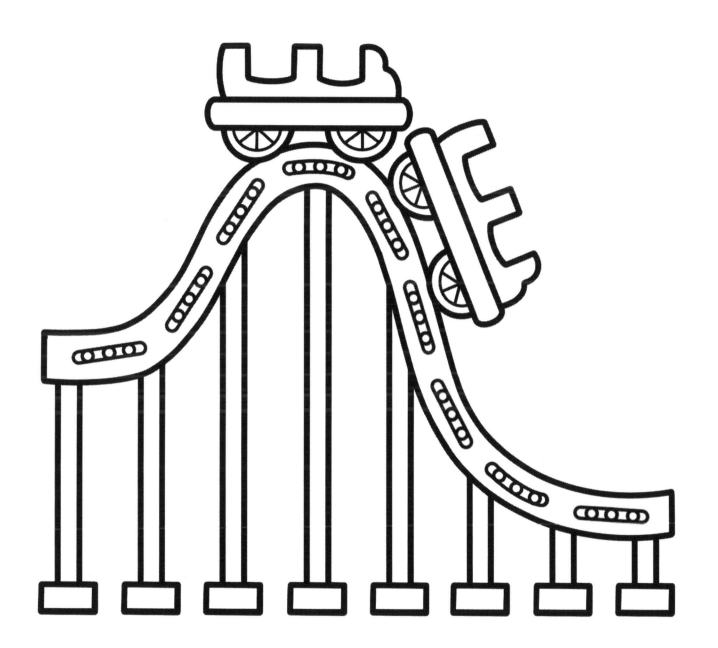

Speak Now

TAYLOR'S VERSION

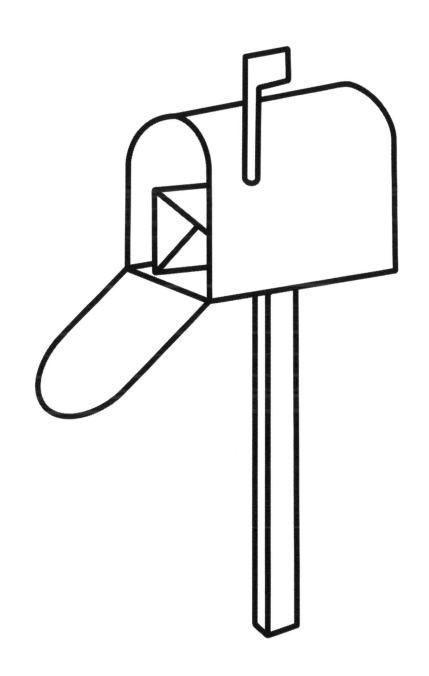

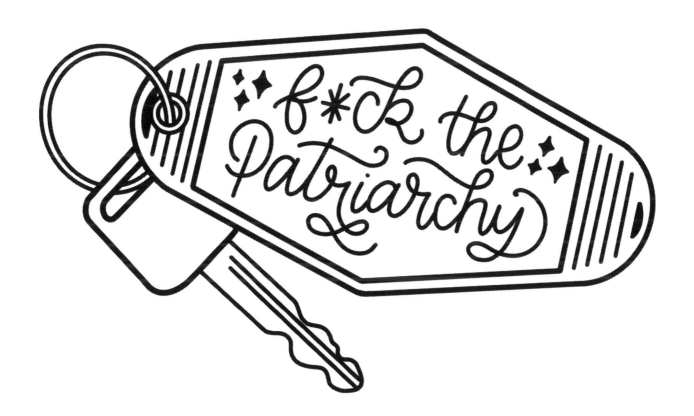

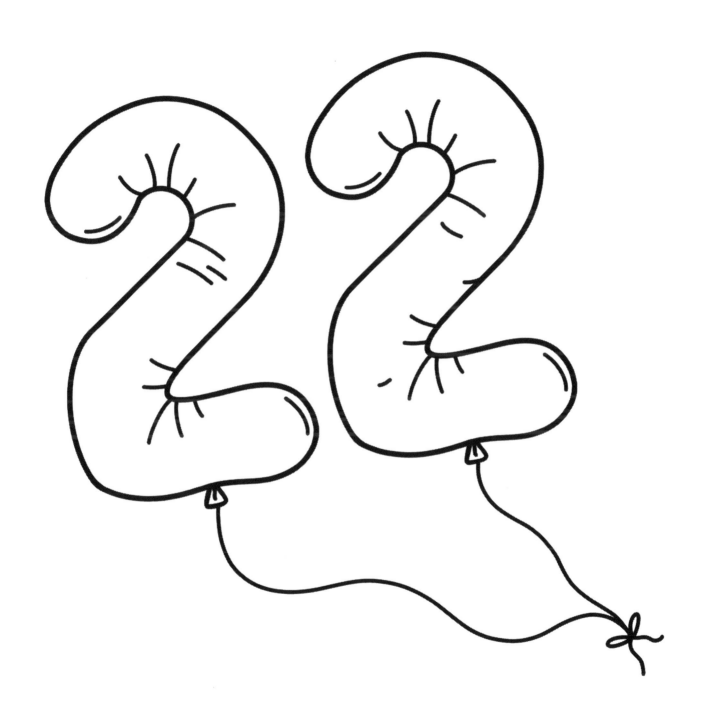

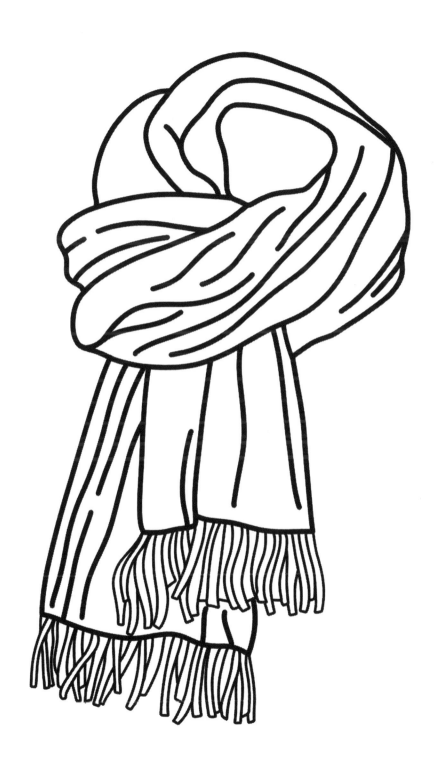

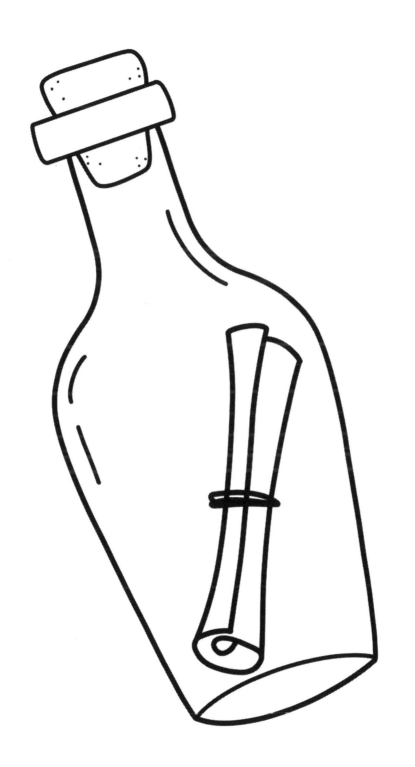

A LOT GOING ON AT THE MOMENT

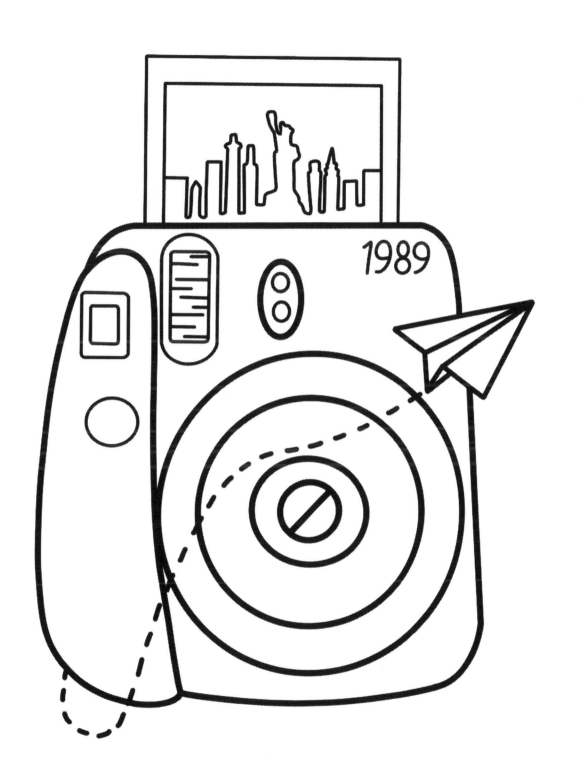

You two are dancing in a snow globe round and round

BLIND FOR LOVE

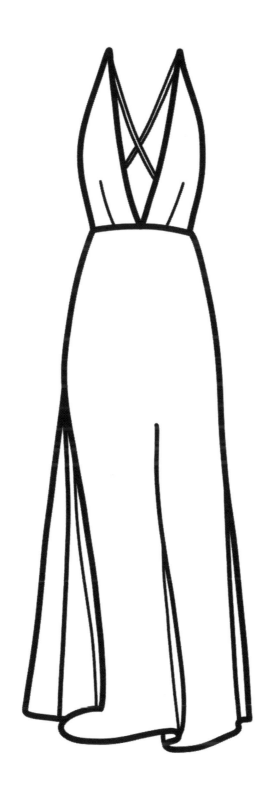

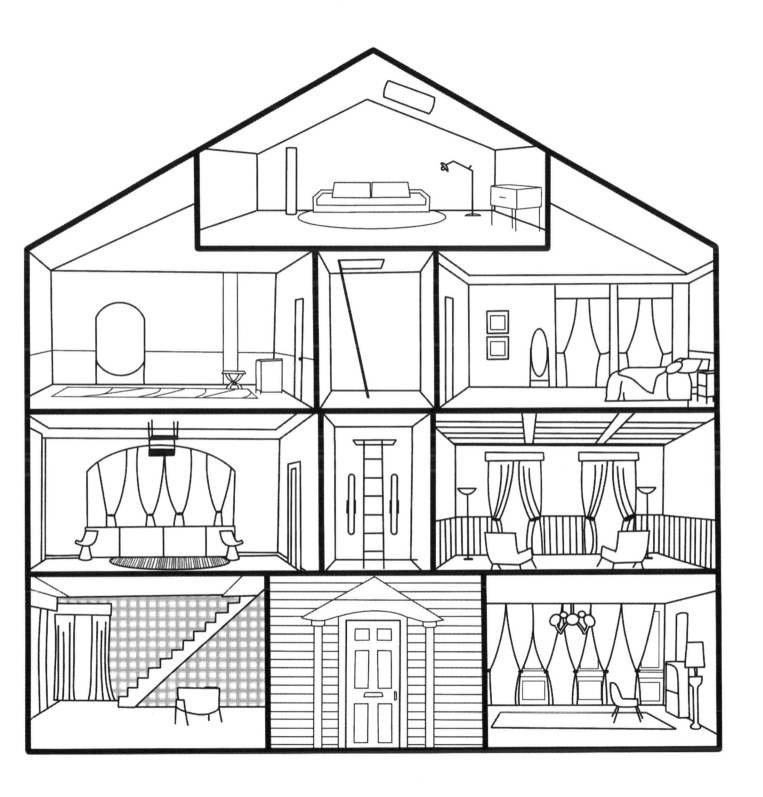

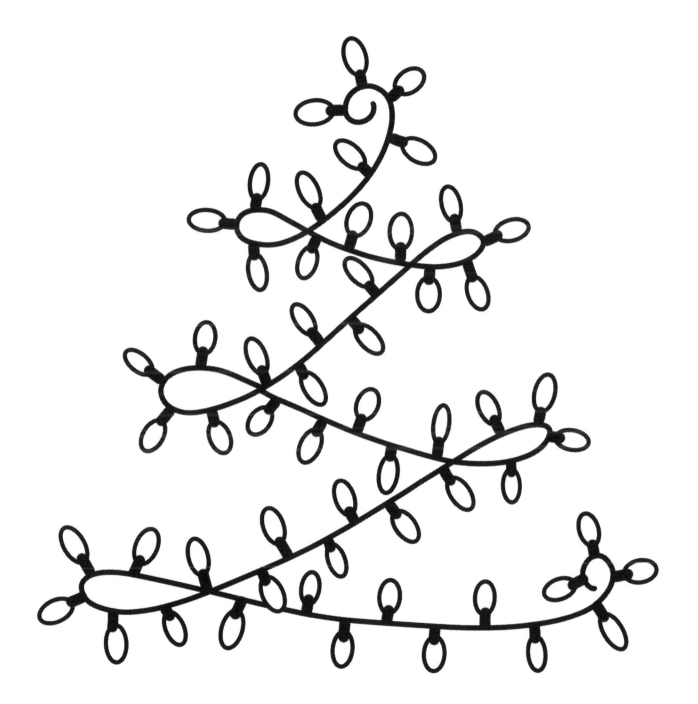

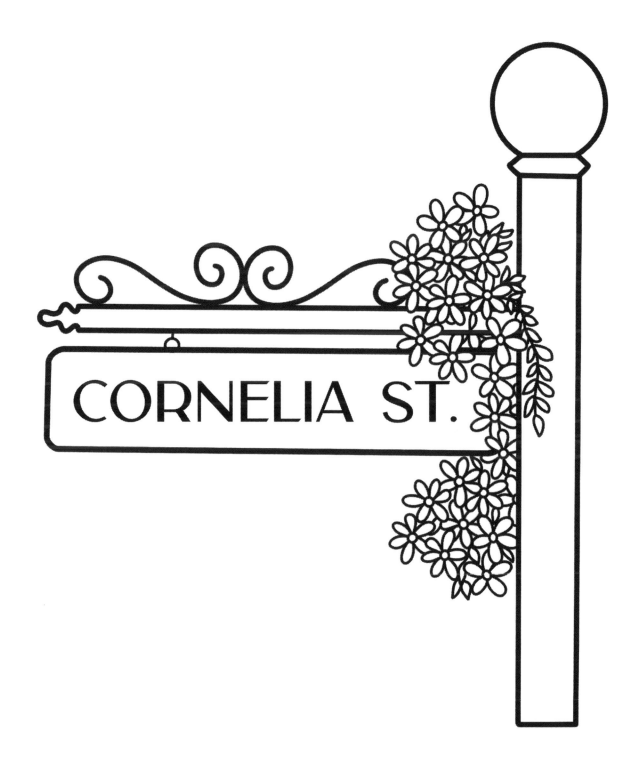

but it's you and me that's my whole world it's been a long time coming

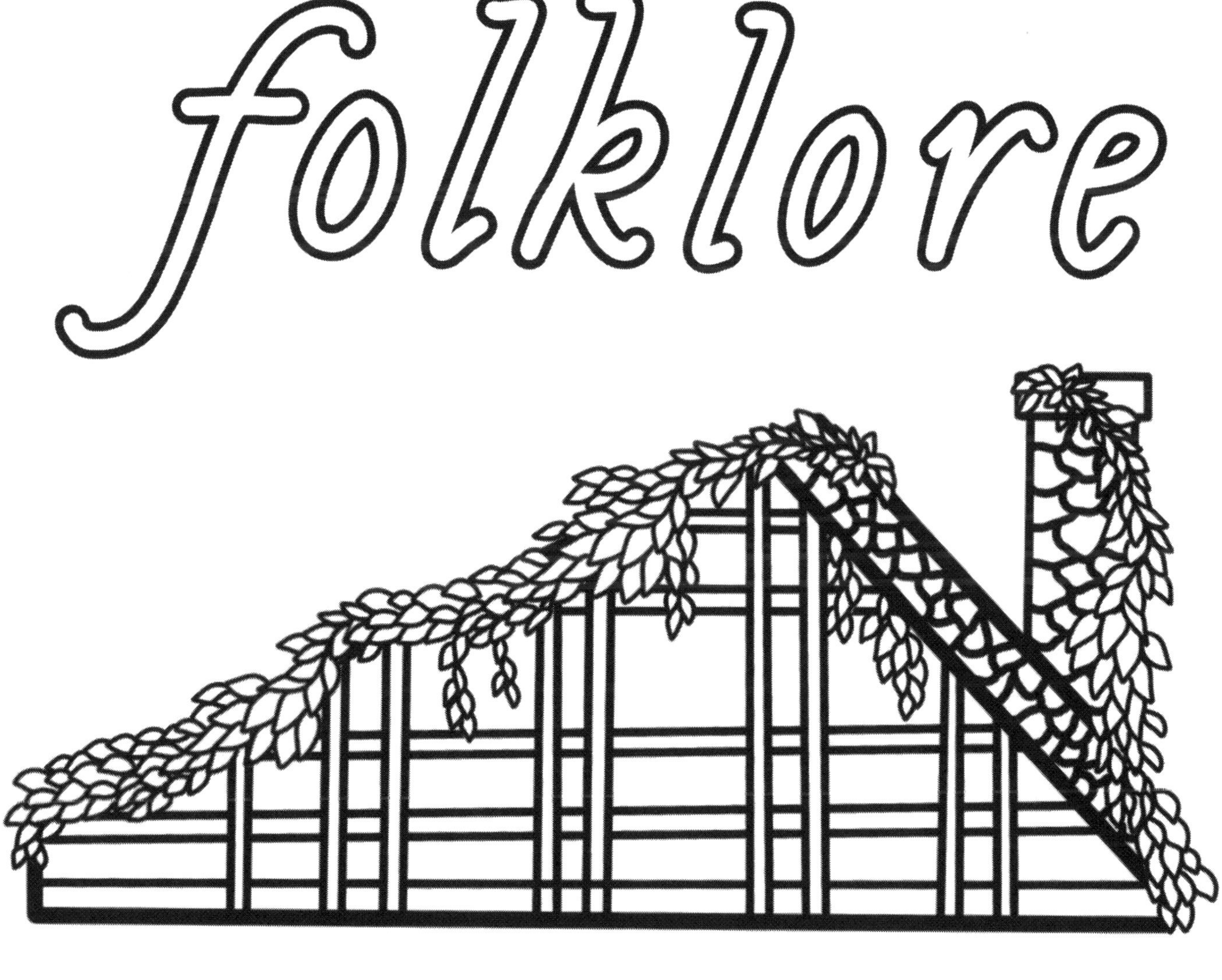
folklore

PRODUCTION *Exile ft. Bon Iver*

SCENE	TAKE
13	1

DIRECTOR *Taylor Swift*

CAMERA *Folklore*

DATE *7/24/2020*

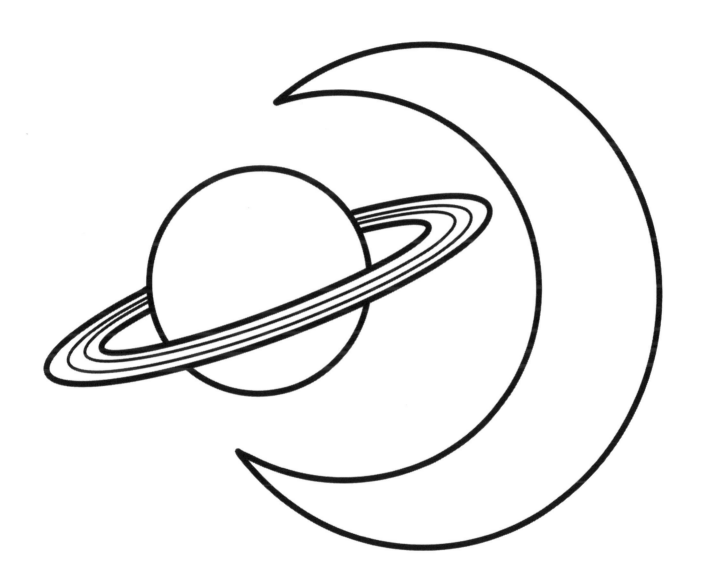

evermore

MIDNIGHTS

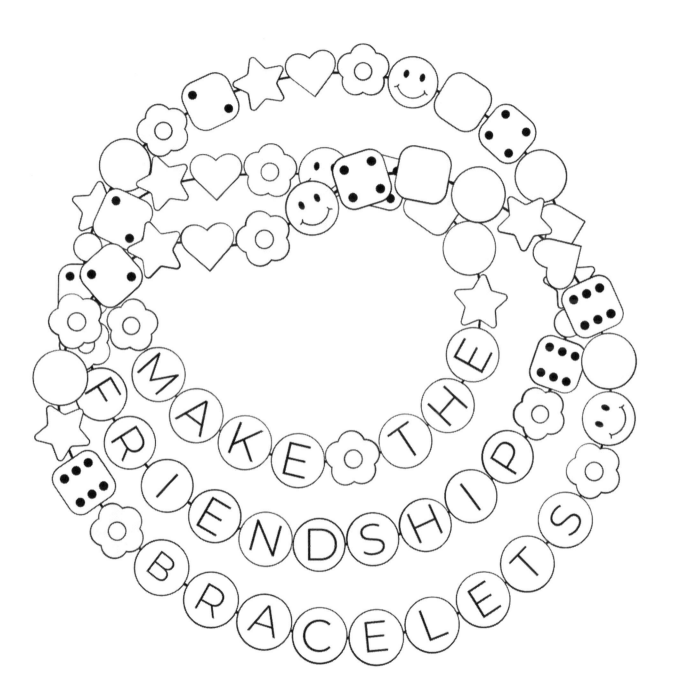

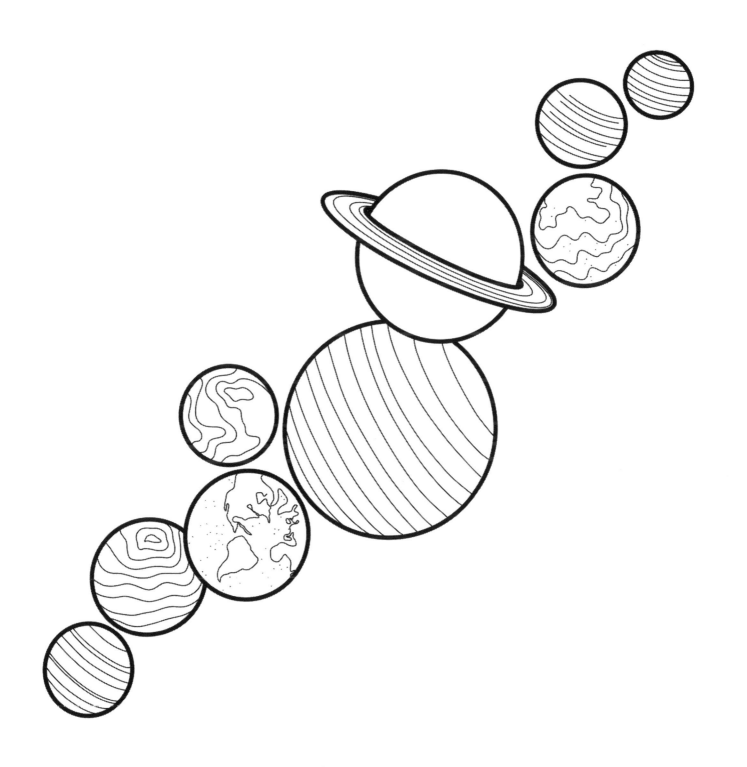

TTPD

ALL'S FAIR IN
LOVE AND POETRY

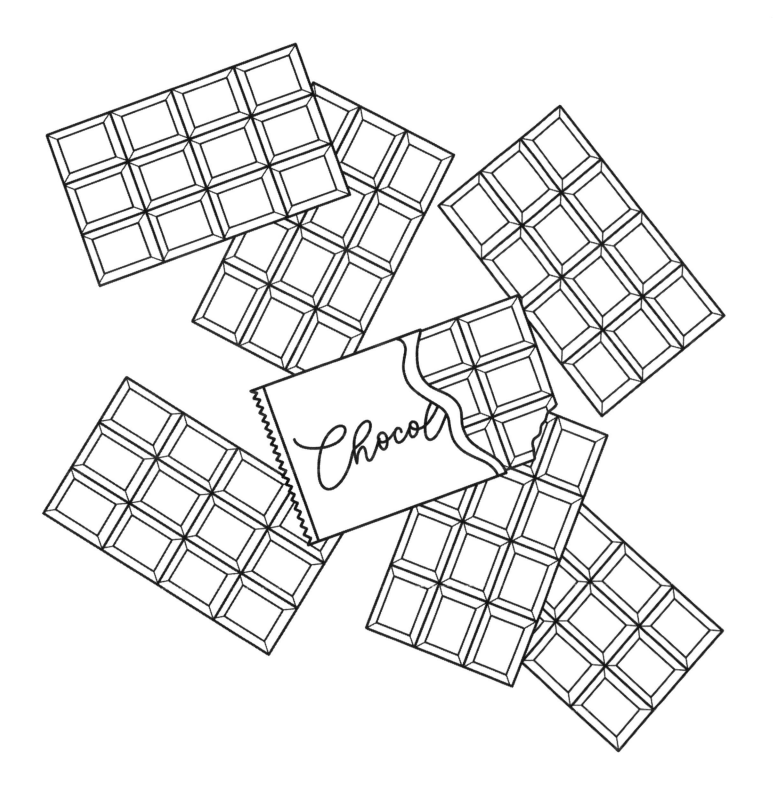

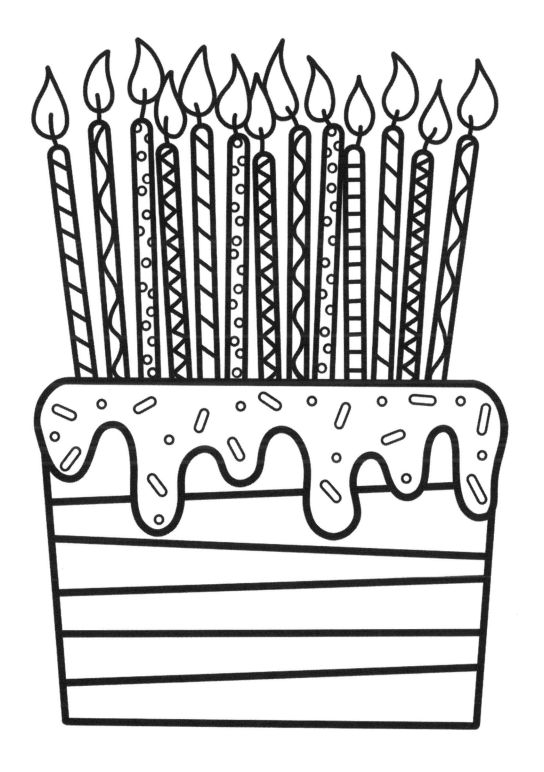

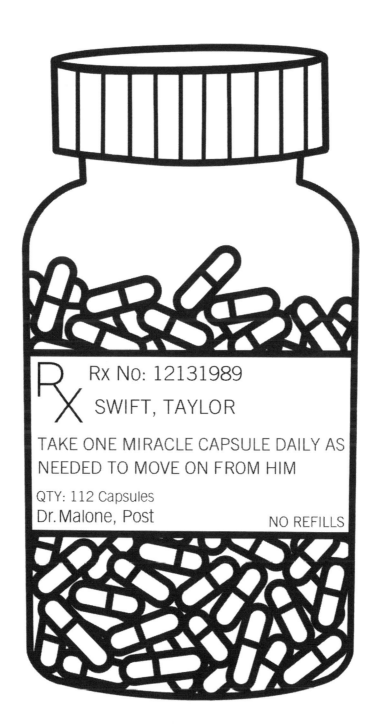

Rx No: 12131989

SWIFT, TAYLOR

TAKE ONE MIRACLE CAPSULE DAILY AS
NEEDED TO MOVE ON FROM HIM

QTY: 112 Capsules
Dr. Malone, Post

NO REFILLS

So Long, London.

London boy

112 Vauxhall Walk, London

SE11 5ER